Zoom in on the US FLAG

ZOOM in on American Symbols

Cecelia H. Brannon

Enslow Publishing
101 W. 23rd Street
Suite 240
New York, NY 10011
USA
enslow.com

WORDS TO KNOW

colonist A person who lives in a new country.

constellation A group of stars that make a pattern or image.

embassy A place where people represent their own country in a foreign country.

horizontal Side by side with the horizon, level with the ground.

perseverance Working hard to do something, despite facing difficulty.

protest A statement or action that shows disapproval.

seamstress A woman whose job is sewing.

secede To stop being a member.

symbol A thing that stands in or represents something else.

upholsterer Someone who makes fabric covering for furniture.

valor Great courage in the face of danger, especially in battle.

CONTENTS

George Washington and his troops gather at Valley Forge during the Revolutionary War.

Stars and Stripes Forever

In 1776, the American colonies were fighting to be free from Great Britain. The colonists needed a symbol of the new nation they were trying to form. They wanted something to look up to and to show that they were separate from the British. A flag was a very good way to do that.

Fighting Britain

The Revolutionary War was fought between the American colonies and Great Britain, but in 1778 France joined in on the side of the colonists. After that, many other countries also joined in to fight against Britain.

Flags Before the Flag

One of the first flags was the famous "Don't Tread on Me" flag, which some people say was designed by Benjamin Franklin. The flag showed a snake atop the words "Don't Tread on Me." There were two designs: one with a yellow background, and one with a red and white striped background. This flag was a protest against the British treatment of the colonists. It

The Grand Union flag

inspired the American colonists to stick up for themselves.

Search for the Flag

On January 1, 1776, George Washington, the general of the Continental Army, began the search for an official flag. While trying to free Boston from British rule, he raised a flag known as the "Grand Union" flag, which had red and white stripes with a union jack (the British flag) in the corner. It was not the first official flag of the United States, but it was the first time colonists had declared themselves separate from the British.

The First Flag

The famous first flag of the United States of America was most likely designed by Francis Hopkinson, a New Jersey congressman and signer of the Declaration of Independence. Many people believe that Betsy Ross, a seamstress and upholsterer, sewed the first American flag. Ross passed that story along to her children and grandchildren, but no one has been able to prove that she made the first flag.

In the early years, there was no rule for where the stars on the flag should go. This hand-sewn flag is from the mid-1800s.

The first flag had thirteen stripes of red and white, and thirteen stars on a blue background. Each star and stripe represented the thirteen colonies that would become a new nation. In the early years, flag makers decided how to arrange the stars. Some placed them in rows while others formed a circle.

The Original Thirteen

At the time that the first flag was made, there were thirteen colonies. They were Delaware, Pennsylvania, New Jersey, Georgia, Connecticut, Massachusetts, Maryland, South Carolina, New Hampshire, Virginia, New York, North Carolina, and Rhode Island.

Making It Official

As the Revolutionary War went on, the flag became a symbol

of hope for many Americans. In 1777 the Continental Congress decided the flag would be "thirteen stripes, alternate red and white; that the union be thirteen stars, white in a blue field, representing a new Constellation."

An early flag shows the 3-2-3-2-3 arrangement of the thirteen stars.

Each of the flag's colors has meaning. Red symbolizes hardiness and valor. White represents purity and innocence. And blue stands for vigilance, perseverance, and justice.

A Changing Flag for a Changing Nation

After the Revolution, the United States became its own nation. The country soon began to grow. By 1795, two more states, Vermont and Kentucky, had been added, so two more stars had to be added to the flag. It was decided the original thirteen stripes would remain, as a reminder that the nation had started small.

"The Star-Spangled Banner"

In 1812, Americans had to defend themselves against the British again. At the Battle of Baltimore in Maryland, British troops tried to take over Fort McHenry. For over twenty-five hours, they bombed the fort. However, they lost. The sight of the American flag still flying over the fort inspired Francis Scott Key to write the poem that would one day be the national anthem: "The Star-Spangled Banner."

More Stars for More States

As the United States became larger and more states joined, more and more stars had to be added. By 1861 there were thirty-four stars on the flag. But this was another

difficult time for the nation. The Civil War had begun, and eleven states seceded from the Union, wishing to create their own country. But President Abraham Lincoln refused to let the nation split. He even refused to remove stars from the flag, despite the fact that

Abraham Lincoln led the United States through the Civil War and was killed just days after it officially ended.

Old Glory

Old Glory is a common nickname for the US flag. It was a name given by William Driver, a sea captain from Massachusetts who lived in the South during the Civil War. He refused to fly the Confederate flag and instead flew his Union flag proudly over his home. Many times throughout the war, Confederates tried to destroy the flag. But it survived the war, and "Old Glory" saw the nation whole again.

the Southern states were calling themselves the Confederate States of America and had their own flag.

The flag continued to change as the nation did. After the Civil War, a thirty-six state flag had to be created for the additions of West Virginia and Nevada. And it continued this way as the nation grew for another hundred years.

The Flag Today

The American flag as we know it today was officially adopted on July 4, 1960, when Hawaii became the last state to join the United States of America. There is a proposed flag with fifty-one stars, in case another state is added.

How to Treat and Display the Flag

The flag must be handled and treated in a certain way. In 1942, President Roosevelt approved the guidelines for the treatment of the flag:

Children take part in a Flag Day parade. These celebrations take place across the country every year on June 14.

- The flag may be displayed from sunrise until sunset every day, unless it is raining or snowing. It must be raised quickly, and lowered with care.
- The flag must be displayed near the main entrances to public and government buildings and polling places during an election. During the week (school days), every school must fly a flag.
- When displayed flat or hung on a wall, the stars must be to the left as a person is looking at it.
- The flag may never be dipped in anyone's direction, or touch the ground. It must always be held horizontally.
- When the flag is part of a ceremony or passes by in a parade, everyone (except those in uniform) should face the flag and put their right hand over their heart.

Places Where the Flag Always Flies

There are a few places where the US flag must fly day and night, even during bad weather:

Fort McHenry (Baltimore, Maryland)
Flag House Square (Baltimore, Maryland)
On the Green of the Town (Lexington, Massachusetts)
The White House (Washington, DC)
National Memorial Arch (Valley Forge, Virginia)
US Marine Corps Memorial (Arlington, Virginia)
All US Customs ports of entry

One Flag, Many Places

The American flag has been in many places outside the United States. Not only is it flown at every US embassy in every country across the world, but it has also been planted in many other places.

In 1909, explorer Robert Peary planted the American flag his wife had sewn at the North Pole. In 1945, US marines raised a flag in Iwo Jima, showing they had beaten the Japanese army and ended World War II. Probably the most famous planting of the flag occurred in 1969, when the crew of Apollo 11 placed the American flag on the moon.

Astronaut Buzz Aldrin stands next to the first American flag on the moon.

ACTIVITY
LEARN HOW TO FOLD A FLAG

Do you know how to fold a flag correctly? Find a friend and practice these steps.

1. With another person, hold the flag waist-high so that its surface is parallel to the ground.

2. Fold the flag in half lengthwise, placing lower half of the flag (the stripes) over the blue and white field of stars.

3. Fold the flag lengthwise again, so that the blue field is on the outside.

4. Make a triangular fold by bringing the corner of the striped corner up to meet the top of the flag (the open part).

5. Turn the point inward parallel to the open edge.

6. Continue folding in this manner. When the flag is completely folded, the field of blue will be the only thing visible.

LEARN MORE

Books

Ferry, Joseph. *American Flag: The Story of Old Glory*. Broomall, PA: Mason Crest, 2014.

Harness, Cheryl. *Flags Over America: A Star-Spangled Story*. Park Ridge, IL: Albert Whitman & Co., 2014.

Monroe, Tyler. *The American Flag*. North Mankato, MN: Capstone Press, 2013.

Websites

PBS

www.pbs.org/a-capitol-fourth/history/old-glory/

History, information, and details about the US flag.

USFlag.org

www.usflag.org/index.html

The official site of the US flag.

INDEX

Published in 2017 by Enslow Publishing, LLC.
101 W. 23rd Street, Suite 240, New York, NY 10011

Library of Congress Cataloging-in-Publication Data

Names: Brannon, Cecelia H., author.

Title: Zoom in on the US flag / Cecelia H. Brannon.

Description: New York, NY : Enslow Publishing, 2017. | Series: Zoom in on American symbols | Includes bibliographical references and index. | Audience: K to grade 3. | Audience: 7-up.

Identifiers: LCCN 2016021448 | ISBN 9780766084605 (library bound) | ISBN 9780766084582 (pbk.) | ISBN 9780766084599 (6-pack)

Subjects: LCSH: Flags—United States—History—Juvenile literature.

Classification: LCC CR113 .B823 2016 | DDC 929.9/20973—dc23

LC record available at https://lccn.loc.gov/2016021448

Printed in China

Photos Credits: Cover, p. 1 (inset flag) Mark Cunningham/Getty Images; cover, p. 1 (background flag) Stillfx/Shutterstock.com; p. 4 Education Images/Universal Images Group/Getty Images; p. 7 Yuriy Boyko/Shutterstock.com; p. 9 © Collection of the New-York Historical Society, USA/ Bridgeman Images; p. 11 MPI/Archive Photos/Getty Images; p. 14 Universal History Archive/ Universal Images Group/Getty Images; p. 17 © Richard Levine/Alamy Stock Photo; p. 21 Time & Life Pictures/The LIFE Picture Collection/Getty Images; p. 23 AbleKane/iStock/Thinkstock; interior pages graphic elements amtitus/DigitalVision Vectors/Getty Images (flag page borders), funnybank/DigitalVision Vectors/Getty Images (flag in circle), gyener/DigitalVision Vectors/ Getty Images (silhouetted flag).